Amgueddfa Genedlaethol Cymru
National Museum of Wales

Cardiff 1976

Welsh Medieval Paving Tiles

This booklet is written by Mr. J. M. Lewis of the
Department of Archaeology at the National Museum of
Wales.

ACKNOWLEDGEMENTS

The photographs are by Mr Eric Broadbent, the book design by Mr Richard Thomas, the kiln drawing by Mr Paul Jenkins, the map by Mr Colin Williams and the reconstruction of the pottery mortar from Denbigh by Mrs M. Hart, all of the National Museum of Wales. The author would also like to thank the Dean and Chapter of Bangor Cathedral for allowing him to draw the Bangor pavement; the County Museum, Carmarthen and the Department of the Environment for permission to photograph tiles in their charge, from Whitland and Basingwerk respectively; Mr G. M. Griffiths, Department of Manuscripts and Records, National Library of Wales; and Penguin Books Ltd.

INTRODUCTION

Y nen fawr uchel yn y nef wreichion
Goruwch, yng ngolwg archangylion;
Y llawr, i bobloedd holl wŷr Bablon
Obry a weithiwyd â main brithion.

The vast high roof in the sparkling heaven above in the sight of
archangels; the floor beneath, for the people of all the men of Babel, is
wrought of variegated stone.

Ode to Lleision, Abbot of Neath
Lewys Morgannwg c. 1500

Floors paved with earthenware tiles began to appear in Britain early
in the thirteenth century, and continued to be fashionable until the
sixteenth century or later. They remained too expensive ever to come
into general use. Most rooms, even in quite affluent houses,
continued to be floored with beaten earth or mortar, with rushes to
give some insulation and a renewable surface that could be changed
when necessary, while great buildings, if it could be afforded, were
floored in marble in imitation of the Italian style. The introduction of
earthenware tiles offered a middle way, and building accounts show
from about 1250 their increasing use in cathedrals, abbeys and churches,
palaces, manors and town houses.

Ceramic tiles were not a European invention, nor were they new in the
thirteenth century. Tin-glazed tiles had been introduced into Spain by
the Moors, but these, with their brilliant pale colours – white, blue,
green and yellow, were very different from the North European
product. The latter, made of the local iron-rich clay covered with a
lead glaze, were red-brown in colour, the white pipe-clay pattern
that often decorated their surfaces standing out as yellow under the
glaze. Yet, laid in contrasting panels enclosed and divided by bands
of plain tiles of dark green or brown, their effect could be striking.
We are familiar with their general effect from the floors of nineteenth
century churches and restorations of the Gothic Revival, but Victorian
technology was too efficient – the texture too regular and the designs
too monotonously uniform – to come close to the authentic medieval
effect.

Innumerable tiles, whole or fragmentary, have survived. A few areas
of pavement still survive intact, but these are comparatively rare. The
vast majority of tiles have long been removed from their pavements, and
exist loose as museum specimens or collectors' pieces.

Their interest as archaeological specimens is threefold. They are
examples of medieval technology and products of a vanished economic
system. There are many questions about their manufacture and
distribution that one would like answered, and, in the absence of
documentary evidence, a study of the tiles themselves is the only way
of answering some of them. But apart from enquiries of this kind,
which must treat all surviving tiles statistically as a single body of
evidence to be quantified and analysed, the individual tile and its
design is often well worth consideration, for, as contemporary products
made by craftsmen for clients, they reflect the tastes and preoccupations
of their times.

In spite of the title of this picture-book, there is nothing particularly
Welsh about the tiles illustrated here, beyond the fact that they were
used in Welsh buildings. We have the evidence of a kiln found at
Denbigh to show that tiles were made in Wales in the Middle Ages,
but it is not possible to point to any of the types or designs as being
of specifically Welsh character or origin. The tile-wright seems to have
been a mobile contractor, prepared to set up a kiln at any building-site
where his products were in demand, whether in England, Wales,
Scotland or Ireland. In this context national frontiers have little relevance,
and evidence from Wales indicates that the tilers employed here came
mainly from Wessex, or Cheshire, or, later, the west Midlands of England.

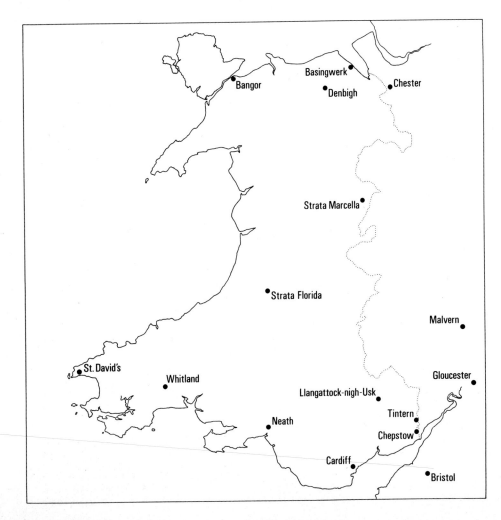

Bangor

Basingwerk

Chester

Denbigh

Strata Marcella

Strata Florida

Malvern

St. David's

Whitland

Gloucester

Llangattock-nigh-Usk

Tintern

Neath

Chepstow

Cardiff

Bristol

PLAIN TILE MOSAICS

The earliest English tile pavements were mosaics made up of tiles of different shapes. There were fine pavements of this type in some of the Cistercian abbeys of Yorkshire – Rievaulx, Byland and Meaux, so that it is not surprising that the Cistercian house at Basingwerk should have produced evidence of one.

These pavements were ultimately derived from Roman pavements of the type known as *opus sectile,* in which pieces of different coloured marbles were laid in a regular pattern. This style was revived in the eleventh century at the monastery of Monte Cassino, and the fashion spread from there to Rome and further afield. At Durham in the twelfth century men going on pilgrimage were asked to bring back pieces of foreign marble for paving, and a pavement of this style was laid at Canterbury about 1200, when the remains of Thomas Becket were removed to their new shrine. The translation of the style into the new medium of earthenware tiles probably took place about this time.

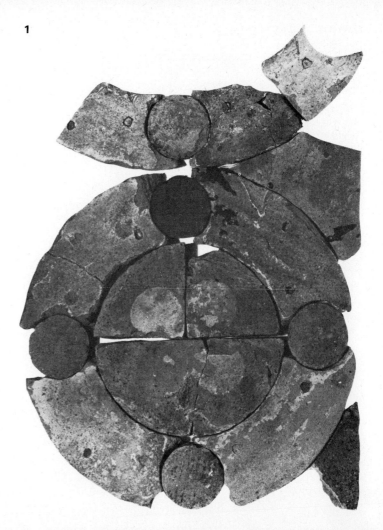

1 *Section of tiles mosaic found during excavation at* **Basingwerk Abbey, Clwyd.** *The effect did not depend on the shapes alone: some are coated with a 'slip' of white clay, and the centre of the circle has a surface decoration of a simple flower pattern in the same technique.*

Mosaic pavements were to regain popularity in certain areas at a later date (see **35**), but this early style was soon replaced by pavements made up of patterned squares, which were more adaptable in filling spaces, and easier to lay.

TYPES OF DECORATION

Pavements of plain, square tiles are not unknown, but most tiles were decorated. Three techniques of decoration were used.

2

2 *Some tiles were impressed with a linear design and then glazed. The whole of the surface was sometimes given a coating of white clay 'slip' under the glaze, but in these cases no attempt was made to differentiate the pattern.*
Strata Marcella Abbey, Powys

3 *The commonest method of decoration was to impress the blank tile with a pattern of deep sunken areas, which were then filled with white clay. When this had dried sufficiently, the surface of the tile was scraped so that the white design stood out in sharp contrast. A lead glaze was then applied before firing.*
Tintern Abbey, Gwent

An extension of this 'inlay' technique is seen in *printed* tiles, where a white clay 'slip' of creamy consistency was applied to the stamp, so that the pattern was left as a thin deposit on the surface of the tile, or slightly sunken into it. The result was not as sharp or as hard wearing, but the method greatly simplified manufacture, and was more widely adopted as tiled floors gained in popularity in the fifteenth century.

Sometimes the white filling was not applied, even in patterns that were clearly meant to have it (**18**), and examples are not infrequent of tiles with the same design, one with and the other without inlay.

4 *A less common technique was to stamp the tile with a design which stood out in relief above a sunken background. The designs of some tiles of this category, like the one illustrated, are carefully modelled, and can truly be called 'embossed.'*
Whitland Abbey, Dyfed

3

4

TILE MANUFACTURE

The sites of tileries, including the kilns and their associated workshops, have been excavated, but relatively little is known with certainty about the details of tile manufacture. When the clay had been prepared it was rolled and cut into blanks of a uniform size. The design was then impressed on to the surface with a wooden stamp. In the case of inlaid tiles the surface was then covered with a white clay 'slip' of a creamy consistency, which filled the impressions in the tile face. When this had dried, the surface of the tile was scraped down to the red clay, so that the white pattern stood out sharply. The face of the tile was then dipped, or painted with a lead glaze, and the tile allowed to dry once again before firing.

5

5 *Reconstructed mortar made of pottery, perhaps for grinding the materials for glazes, found on the site of the Denbigh kiln. (Diameter 11.5 cm).*

6 *In 1938 a tile kiln, probably of the fourteenth century, came to light in **Middle Lane, Denbigh** during building operations. This reconstruction drawing shows the kiln as it might have looked when in use. It is very similar to kilns found in Chester, and seems to have produced roof tiles, though a tile of a known Chester design was also found on the site, so that it might have been producing floor tiles as well. Firing would have been by wood or peat. Excavations have shown that such kilns probably did not have permanent roofs, but temporary ones, sealed with clay, which were built after the kiln had been stacked. The method of stacking tiles in the kiln illustrated here is conjectural, but seems the best way of stacking tiles with bevelled edges, as so many of them were.*

TILE PAVEMENTS

Tile pavements were laid on a bed of lime mortar: they sometimes have hollows scooped underneath to help key them. Their edges are often bevelled, so that they could be laid edge to edge with the minimum of gaps at the surface.

Patterned tiles were not laid haphazardly, but were organised into carpet designs. Single tiles often formed parts of geometrical patterns covering large areas of floor between contrasting borders; sometimes a floor was divided into decorative panels separated by plain tile strips.

Very few areas of pavement remain *in situ* in Wales. There is part of a fifteenth century floor at St David's Cathedral, and at Bangor Cathedral a small area of fourteenth century pavement has been relaid from tiles found during restoration. Small areas of pavement, uncovered during the summer months each year, can be seen in the ruins of Neath, St Dogmael's, Strata Florida and Talley Abbeys.

7

DAIS RISING ABOUT FOUR INCHES.

8

10

7 *Four-tile design from* **Tintern Abbey**. *13th century.*

8 *Area of 14th century floor found at* **Neath Abbey, West Glamorgan**, *in 1833. The tiles forming the geometrical pattern are closely similar to* **2** *in design; for the hunting scene border, see* **17**.

9 *Many pavements include circular designs made up of four, nine or sixteen tiles. This area of 14th century paving at* **Neath Abbey** *shows how a sixteen-tile pattern could be extended into a symmetrical design of sixty-four tiles, or even more.*

CLARENDON PALACE AND THE WESSEX SCHOOL

One of the factors that helped to establish the fashion of tiled floors in the thirteenth century was their use in royal buildings erected under the direction of King Henry III, who took a personal interest in the planning of buildings, down to the details of their decoration.

One of the pavements best documented in the royal accounts is the one laid in the Queen's Chamber at Clarendon Palace, near Salisbury, in 1250-1. This pavement is also of importance for understanding the way the craft developed in the west of England and south Wales. When the work at Clarendon was finished, the same tilers seem to have worked at Salisbury and Winchester, and before long what can be seen as a 'Wessex School' had become established, using a common repertory of patterns, including designs copied or derived from the Clarendon pavement of 1250. These designs, differing only in minor details from the originals, are found across south Wales as far west as Kidwelly Castle, implying perhaps the presence of itinerant contractors following where the demand for their services led them.

10

10
11
12

*These three tiles from **Tintern Abbey** are closely similar to some from the Queen's Chamber at Clarendon, though at Clarendon the lion and griffin face each other in pairs. They are typical of the kind of exotic animal designs that were being introduced into England at this time, their immediate source being eastern textiles from Byzantium, Damascus or Sicily. Many found their way into heraldry. Such fabrics would have been most familiar as church vestments: a 13th century chasuble, said to have belonged to Margaret de Clare, wife of Edmund Plantagenet, is embroidered with opposed lions and griffins in a way reminiscent of these tiles.*

11

12

13

In 1250 Henry III ordered a wall painting of 'the combat of King Richard' for the chamber under the chapel at Clarendon Palace. Crusading subjects were much to the king's taste, and it was natural that he should have wished to include this episode, albeit legendary, involving his illustrious uncle. Richard I (Richard *Coeur de Lion*), who had spent so much of his reign crusading, seems to have become a popular hero within a short time of his death in 1189, one of the many legends that grew up round him being concerned with his meeting in single combat with the Saracen leader, Saladin, variously described as taking place at the Battle of Arsour or before the gates of Babylon. This episode, in which heathen cunning is overcome by the superior Christian variety, has come down to us in a popular verse romance of

the 14th century, and was also the subject of a set of paving tiles of superb quality from Chertsey Abbey, which King Henry might have presented to the Abbey in the 1270s. It was also among the subjects illustrated on Wessex tiles, where it exists in several versions that differ in minor points of detail.

13 *This pair of 14th century tiles from* **Neath Abbey** *depict two mounted knights, one armed with shield and lance, the other with scimitar and round buckler, which are enough to identify him as Saladin, though they lack many points of detail that are included in the literary version of the story.*

Another common Wessex subject consisted of a symmetrical design of two birds feeding off the branches of a tree. Some treatments are extremely conventional, others more naturalistic. The design, like others, may have been derived from textiles.

14

14 St John's Church, Cardiff
This version is very widespread in Wessex, being found at Salisbury Cathedral, Winchester Castle and Glastonbury Abbey, which offers the closest parallel to this tile from south Wales.

15 Tintern Abbey, Gwent
Another widespread version with many local variants. The closest parallel to this tile from Tintern is from Cleeve Abbey, Somerset.

16 Strata Florida Abbey, Powys
A devolved local version of the same subject.

15

16

17

SCENES FROM MEDIEVAL LIFE

Throughout the Middle Ages hunting was a favourite pastime of the nobility. Apart from being considered enjoyable it was regarded as a suitable exercise and training in the lordly virtues, and an elaborate lore and ritual developed around it.

In a stag hunt relays of dogs stationed on the probable course of the run were used to drive the animal towards the hunting party, who shot at it with bows and arrows, while other relays were placed round the area of the hunt to prevent the animals escaping.

Always harried by hounds hard on their heels,
And the hurrying hunters' high horn notes.
Like the rending of ramped hills roared the din.
If one of the wild beasts slipped away from the archers
It was dragged down and met death at the dog bases
After being hunted from the high ground and harried to the water,
So skilled were the hunt-servants at stations lower down,
So gigantic the greyhounds that grabbed them in a flash,
Seizing them savagely, as swift, I swear,
As sight.

Sir Gawain and the Green Knight (14th century)

* Sir Gawain and the Green Knight, *trans. Brian Stone, second edition, 1974, lines 1164–1172 (Reprinted by permission of Penguin Books Ltd).*

17 *The incident depicted on this 14th century tile from* **Neath Abbey**
*seems to represent the kind of incident described in the above
passage. The greyhounds are bringing down the runaway stag, closely
pursued by the pack of running-hounds, while the kennel-man
in charge of the relay of dogs blows a warning signal on his horn,
slung on a baldrick round his neck.*

18

18 Strata Florida Abbey, Powys
*This tile can be dated to the 14th century by the costume of the man,
who wears a doublet buttoned to below his waist, with a hip belt and
purse over it; like the figure in the Neath hunting scene he wears a
hood fitting closely round his face, with a long point falling behind his
back, and pendant sleeves. He is shown looking into a mirror, and may
be intended as an allegorical figure representing Pride or Vanity. The
tile has been impressed with a pattern suitable for inlaying with white
clay, but this has been omitted, though an overall white slip has been
applied. This often happens: pairs of tiles from the same stamp have
been found, one with an inlay and one without.*

19

HERALDIC TILES

Tiles decorated with heraldic shields of arms were frequently included in pavements to commemorate founders or benefactors. They form an interesting class of tiles, as they are in this way linked with people and historical events, which is sometimes a help in dating a pavement. On the other hand, they can help to identify benefactors who might not otherwise be known, though the absence of heraldic colours can present difficulties in identification.

19 **Neath Abbey,** *from the 14th century paving of the church.*
(Gules) three clarions (or)* : *these are the arms attributed to Robert Consul, Earl of Gloucester, natural son of Henry I, for the good of whose soul the Abbey was founded by Richard de Granville in 1129.*

20 *Also from* **Neath Abbey**
(Or) three chevrons (gules), *the arms of the de Clare family, who would have had a double qualification for inclusion in a 14th century pavement at Neath: Earl Gilbert de Clare helped the building of the Abbey church in 1298 with a gift of timber, but he was also descended from a grand-daughter of Robert Consul, and so entitled to inclusion as kin of the man in whose honour the Abbey had been founded.*

21 **Tintern Abbey, Gwent**
(Argent) a lion rampant (gules) crowned (or) within a bordure (sable) bezanty : *the arms of Richard of Cornwall (1209-1272), brother of Henry III, or of his son Edmund (d.1300). Both were patrons of the Cistercian Abbey of Hailes, Gloucestershire, from which tiles of this design are also known. Both were related by marriage with the de Clares, Richard having married Isabella, widow of the first Earl Gilbert, and Edmund having married Margaret, the sister of the Earl Gilbert, who was patron of Neath.*

On tiles arms are of necessity depicted in two colours only, but their correct colours are given in the descriptions, in the customary heraldic terms, viz. or (gold), argent (silver), gules (red), sable (black), proper (in its proper colours), azure (blue).

19

20

21

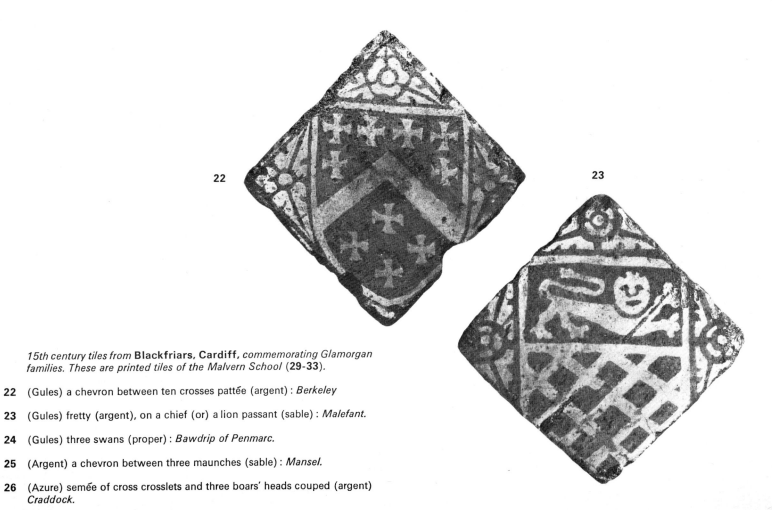

22

23

15th century tiles from **Blackfriars, Cardiff,** *commemorating Glamorgan families. These are printed tiles of the Malvern School* (**29-33**).

22 (Gules) a chevron between ten crosses pattée (argent) : *Berkeley*

23 (Gules) fretty (argent), on a chief (or) a lion passant (sable) : *Malefant.*

24 (Gules) three swans (proper) : *Bawdrip of Penmarc.*

25 (Argent) a chevron between three maunches (sable) : *Mansel.*

26 (Azure) semée of cross crosslets and three boars' heads couped (argent) *Craddock.*

25

24

26

ALPHABET TILES

Some tiles bear letters of the alphabet, and are intended to be combined into inscriptions. Such tiles are found in various parts of the country: at York Minster, in Leicestershire and at Hereford Cathedral, while an inscription from Fladby Church, Worcestershire, can be dated to 1371.

27

27 *These tiles from* **Chepstow, Gwent,** *with letters in the Lombardic style of the 14th century, are the only ones of their type known from Wales.*

28

28 *Border tile with the inscription 'Deus' (God) in Lombardic style, from*
Basingwerk Abbey, Clwyd.

THE MALVERN SCHOOL

In 1455, in the time of Abbot Sebroke, an impressive tile pavement was laid in front of the High Altar in Gloucester Abbey (now the Cathedral). Linked with this pavement are wall-tiles of a similar style, dated 1453 and 1457/8, at Great Malvern Priory. Nineteenth century excavations near the Priory at Malvern uncovered the kiln that had supplied the tiles used in the Church, while another kiln making tiles of the same type was discovered near Droitwich. Tiles with similar patterns are found over a wide area of the Severn Valley and as far west as St David's, so that it is possible to speak of a 'Malvern School'. The tiles are well made and are characterised by complex but well-organised designs, frequently architectural in character and with inscriptions. It is unlikely that they were all made at Malvern: their wide distribution, and minor variations in pattern and size, seem to imply the presence of craftsmen trained at Malvern and following the local tradition, but taking their skills where building work demanded. The most notable example of their work in Wales is at **St David's Cathedral,** and it is worth noting that Bishop Tully of St David's (1460-c.1481) had supervised the building of the splendid tower at Gloucester as a monk under Abbot Sebroke, where he would no doubt have become acquainted with the work of the Malvern tilers.

29

29 *Malvern tiles from the church of* **Llangattock nigh Usk,**
30 *both with designs that occur in Abbot Sebroke's pavement at Gloucester. They are also known from Monmouth.*
    29 the central motif is a crowned Ihc (Jesus).
    30 has the arms of Edward the Confessor and the Abbey of Gloucester, represented by the keys and sword of St Peter.

31 *Unprovenanced Malvern type tile, with typical architectural design.*

30

31

Pavements were not only laid in churches. A pavement closely related to Abbot Sebroke's pavement at Gloucester was laid, probably about 1460, in the house of William Canynges, a merchant of Bristol. It has survived practically intact, and is now in the British Museum. It consists of panels of 4- and 16-tile patterns, separated by bands of plain tiles. It is the pavement with the closest affinity to the one at St David's; it is also closely paralleled at Cardiff.

32
33 *Tiles forming parts of designs similar to those on the Canynges*
34 *pavement, found on the site of* **Lloyd's Bank, High Street, Cardiff** *in 1892. Finds of medieval pottery were also recovered from the same site, but the circumstances of the find were not recorded, so that it is impossible to say whether the tiles were an original feature of the house or a relaid pavement that had originally been at the Cardiff Blackfriars: certainly, fragmentary tiles of the same design were found during excavation at Blackfriars.* **22-26** *belong to the same series.*

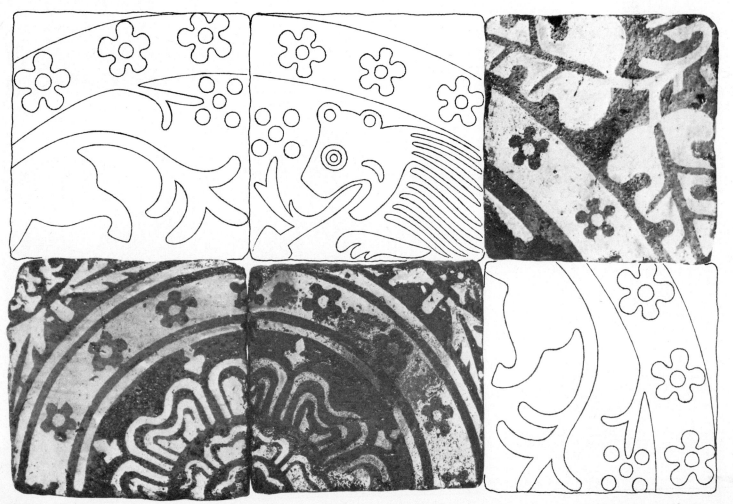

LINE-IMPRESSED TILES

Alongside the inlaid tradition of manufacture went a technically simpler tradition in which tiles were impressed with a linear pattern, but not given a white filling. The tile is sometimes given an overall white slip, but in these cases no attempt is made to differentiate the impressed pattern. One school of tile-wrights working in this tradition flourished in the fourteenth century in Cheshire, and the midland counties of Staffordshire, Shropshire and Derbyshire, perhaps originating at Repton, and their products seem to have spread into north and mid-Wales, and further afield to Dublin. Chester, where tile-making is known to have been carried on, seems, as one might expect, to have been the centre of distribution, as Chester designs are known from several Welsh sites. All tiles with Chester patterns need not, of course, have been made there, but, as in the case of the Wessex and Malvern schools, tilers trained in the Chester tradition, and using the same set of designs, may have set up kilns where and when demand arose.

35

35 *Tile with line-impressed pattern of a griffin, from* **Strata Florida Abbey,** *where it was used as a border tile in the chapels of the south transept, associated with* **18**. *Tiles of this design were also used at Strata Marcella, Montgomery Castle, Norton Priory, Cheshire and St Patrick's Cathedral, Dublin. It was also a popular subject in the Wessex School. The griffin, a winged quadruped with the head of an eagle, was one of the beasts pictured in the medieval* Bestiary, *which supplied the subjects of the pavement in the same technique at Bangor* (**36, 37**).

The most impressive pavements of the line-impressed school were tile mosaics. These represent a revival in a more elaborate form of the type of pavement popular among the Cistercians in the thirteenth century, as represented by the earlier floor at Basingwerk (1). Apart from the addition of line decoration, the new pavements adopted more elaborately shaped panels, which are reminiscent of the embroidery on certain church vestments, and suggest that they may owe something to textile design.

36 *The subject of the later pavement from* **Basingwerk Abbey** (*also found at the Shropshire abbeys of Buildwas, Lilleshall and Wenlock) suggests a further link with church vestments. The angelic winged creature is derived from the prophet's vision found in the first chapter of the book of Ezekiel, which had 'feet like the sole of a calf's foot' and 'the hands of a man under its wings', while the surrounding circles are the wheels, which appeared in the vision as embodying the spirit of the creatures. The subject, a favourite one for vestments over a long period, is to be seen on a cope of c.1260 and again on two copes of c.1500.*

THE BANGOR CATHEDRAL TILES

During Sir Gilbert Scott's restoration of **Bangor Cathedral** in 1869 a
large number of tiles were found loose in debris below the floor of the
Choir and elsewhere. They are now to be seen relaid at the west end
of the north aisle. They belong to the line-impressed tradition of the
north-west, and individual tiles among the finds can be paralleled at
Chester and elsewhere, including Dublin. But as yet no parallels have
anywhere been noted to the remarkable designs illustrated here.

37

37 *Square tiles forming a repeating pattern of two roundels, each
encircled by a border with dragons. The subjects are derived from the
Bestiary,* one of the most popular and influential books of the Middle
Ages. It was first compiled from earlier writers in the 12th century, but
continued to expand with copying throughout the period, so that there
is not one Bestiary, but really as many works as there are copies,
though much of the material is common to them all. It purports to be an
account of the animal world, with descriptions, pictures and an
explanation of the emblematic significance of each beast in terms of
Christian teaching.

The subjects illustrated here are the 'Caladrius', the bird depicted as
perching on the bed of a sick man: if he is going to recover the
caladrius faces him, if not it turns away. It was thought to take the
man's sickness into itself, and to fly up to the sun to disperse it into
the air, thus being regarded as an emblem of Christ.

The pair of heads are probably meant to represent another Bestiary
subject, the 'Terebolem', a mysterious word probably misreading the
Greek for 'fire-darting' stones. The subject in the writer's mind seems to
have been pyrites. In the Bestiary two figures, usually male and female,
are depicted, the mountain peak on which they stand bursting into flames
as the stones they hold in their hands touch. The shape between the
Bangor heads represents a flame. Some versions, as in the Bangor
tiles, seem to make no attempt to differentiate the sex of the figures.
There follows an admonition to the clergy to keep away from women,
'lest the twin-born flame should break out in yourselves and burn up
the good things which Christ has conferred on you'.

38 The other section of pavement at Bangor is an elaborate tile mosaic of
circles divided unusually into seven segments, with central lion faces,
and with lion faces surrounded by conventional foliage designs
between. Again the subjects are animals, though these cannot be as
easily traced to Bestiary sources. They include peacocks, around which a
varied lore had developed: their supposedly incorruptible flesh made
them an emblem of immortality; their cries in the night for fear of losing
their beauty were taken as an emblem of the Christian's fear of falling
from grace; they were thought to feel ashamed and collapse their
splendid tails whenever they looked down at their ugly feet, a salutary
reminder that there is never any justification for Pride. The Lion,
mightiest of beasts, was considered an emblem of Christ.
The design of the hare and the bird is puzzling: it might belong to a
class of whimsical subjects popular in the Middle Ages, in which
familiar roles are reversed, and the hunted becomes the hunter—the
hare here appears to have a rather dangerous looking paw raised to
attack the bird.

RELIEF TILES

Tiles decorated with designs in relief are less common in the Middle Ages than other types. Their comparative unpopularity is understandable, as they would have been most uncomfortable to walk on, and their patterns would have become worn sooner than the flat, inlaid types. Relief tiles are found in widely scattered areas, East Anglia being the only region in which they were widely used. They are known from two sites in Wales: Bangor (from the evidence of a single tile now in the Victoria and Albert Museum) and Whitland Abbey. No parallels are known for the designs from either site, and their presence at both seems likely to be circumstantial rather than the result of the normal course of trade and building operations. The type originated in north Switzerland and the region of the upper Rhine, and the designs seem to be derived from Norman Sicily, where Moslem influence was strong.

39

39 Whitland Abbey, Dyfed
13th century tile with central 'Agnus Dei' symbol surrounded by a border which includes animals and four shields with conventional heraldic devices, probably not intended to have any particular significance. The animals are: a peacock; a bird with a strange clubbed tail, perhaps intended to be a swan; what seems to be a two-headed dragon, perhaps intended to represent an amphisbena, a two-headed reptile that figured in the Bestiary; and a lion.

40

Relief tiles, representing the end of this medieval tradition, were being made in the Barnstaple area of north Devon in the sixteenth and seventeenth centuries. Fragmentary examples of these tiles, including a Tudor rose design; have been found in Cardiff. No doubt more remain to be found along the south Wales coast, where they were probably as popular as the other pottery products of their area.

40 *Tile of North Devon type with Renaissance style head in relief. Provenance unknown.*

SOME FURTHER READING

Elizabeth S. Eames, **Medieval Tiles: a handbook** (British Museum, London 1968)
Arthur Lane, **A Guide to the Collection of Tiles** (Victoria & Albert Museum, London 1939, 2nd edition 1960)
Loyd Haberly, **Mediaeval Pavingtiles** (Oxford 1937)